Plastic Vanitas
Mariele Neudecker

text + work

TheGallery
Arts University Bournemouth

Plastic Vanitas
**A collaborative project and exhibition with TheGallery & MoDiP,
Arts University Bournemouth.**

Published 2015
By text + work, TheGallery, Arts University Bournemouth.

A catalogue record of this publication is available from the British
Library: British Library Cataloguing-in-Publication Data
ISBN: 978-0-901196-67-5

Edited by Susan Lambert and Violet McClean.

Designed by Sally Hope.

A limited edition of 4000 copies is printed for this project.

ARTS
UNIVERSITY
BOURNEMOUTH

Contents

Introduction:
Emma Hunt

The Arts University Bournemouth (AUB) is delighted to introduce *Plastic Vanitas*, the complementary exhibition for our international conference being held in September 2015. The *Provocative Plastics* conference and exhibition were conceived following the work of the Museum of Design in Plastics (MoDiP) in a number of groundbreaking activities that challenged the work of museums in bringing in new audiences whilst maintaining its serious research and conservation remit.

For AUB, the innovative work of MoDiP came as no surprise as this is a University that challenges and invents, and remains at the forefront of arts education by being focused on its values of innovation, connectivity and collaboration. This exhibition and conference display all of these values. The AUB is a specialist university dedicated to the higher education of all subjects falling within art, design, architecture, media and performance disciplines. AUB embraces its Gallery as being central to the visual and written review of all creative subjects through TheGallery programme and associated text + work publications, and has built up an enviable reputation in encouraging students and external visitors to be active members of the gallery resources and debates.

Just as AUB is unique in its focus, so is MoDiP, with its concentration on the everyday objects designed and made in plastics. It maintains its accredited museum status but actively looks at new ways to engage the public and students in its role. Consequently when the *Provocative Plastics* conference idea emerged, it was clear that

the basic premise of 'good' or 'bad' plastics would be perfectly represented in visual terms by the artist Mariele Neudecker who took the conference mantra *your view dictates what you see* to the limits in her beautifully constructed photographs, and adds to the range of viewpoints that will be presented at the conference.

Sometimes the links between a museum, a gallery, a university and the research collaborators from other organisations cannot be as perfectly intertwined as this conference and exhibition demonstrates; they are a clear example of AUB's commitment to collaboration and the new ways of thinking that will emerge.

Mariele Neudecker has been the perfect artist with whom to collaborate and we are equally indebted to the Arts Council England for funding the exhibition, to Bath Spa University for additional support, and to all the exhibition and conference collaborators for making this such an interesting and worthwhile event.

Professor Emma Hunt
Deputy Vice Chancellor
Arts University Bournemouth

Curator's overview
Susan Lambert

Curator's overview
Susan Lambert

Art does not reproduce the visible; rather, it makes visible.
Paul Klee, Creative Credo, 1920

Plastic Vanitas is a series of photographic artworks by Mariele Neudecker that re-presents the collection of the MoDiP collection as vanitas still lifes. MoDiP, the only accredited UK museum with a focus on plastics, is a research resource of the Arts University Bournemouth. Plastic Vanitas was created on-site during the artist's residency. The project and exhibition have been organised in collaboration with TheGallery at the Arts University Bournemouth.

Plastics are now the most used materials group in manufacturing. Plastic things are, therefore, everywhere yet they are mostly invisible. In *Museum without walls* André Malraux pointed out that a Romanesque crucifix was not regarded by its contemporaries as a sculpture; or Cimabue's *Madonna* as a picture; or Phidias's *Pallas Athene* as primarily a statue. They were functional objects like those in the MoDiP collection. He reasoned it was their bringing together in museums that divested them of their functions. Such is the power of the concept of the work of art that now even the sitter in a portrait often takes second place to the artist, the painting becoming a Velazquez, Rembrandt or Titian. MoDiP's collection has, however, seemed proof against such transformation. Rather, people are surprised to find objects more often encountered on supermarket shelves or in department stores spotlit in museum display cases. Although the objects are no longer in use, they tend to retain in the eye of the museum visitor their functional identity. A ketchup dispenser remains a ketchup dispenser; a hair dryer, a hair dryer. While we, too, are interested in the role of the objects as conceived, we also want to open up their meanings and significance.

Mariele Neudecker has been the perfect collaborator. Intensification of the act of looking and seeing is at the heart of what she does. Working in a variety of traditional and new media including time-based sculptural installations, video installations, photographs, drawings and paintings, and objects found, made or manufactured, she uses imagery invented, retrieved and reconsidered from our common cultural consciousness, and represents what we know so we

Fig. 1 Boxed MoDiP objects in store

see it as we have never seen it before.

Vanitas painting is a specific genre of still-life painting that flourished in Flanders and the Netherlands in the sixteenth and seventeenth centuries in which the most exquisite accoutrements of everyday life are presented as symbols of the worthlessness of earthly achievement and the inevitability of death. The vanitas concept thus provides a lens through which to interpret the objects depicted.

Neudecker was fascinated by how MoDiP's collection is stored in anonymous boxes (fig.1) by plastic material, size and weight, seemingly in random accumulations of objects that make no intellectual sense. The featured box contents were selected as a result of the artist listing object types depicted in vanitas paintings: skulls, mirrors, drinking vessels, candles, scales, fruit, flowers, insects and so on and the MoDiP staff selecting some fifty boxes from the

Curator's overview

1000 plus in the collection that contained at least one such object or something physically similar. For example, there are no skulls but there are crash helmets and they take a similar form, and thus can act as substitutes. The rest was left to intuition and the artist's alchemy. Each photographic artwork includes every object that is stored in the particular box housing the selected object. Objects stored singly are re-presented in isolation.

The resulting images are remarkable. They are also beautiful. The vanitas paradigm shines a new light literally and metaphorically on these mundane objects. Individually they are redefined as contributors to life's precarious mortality. Clocks (fig.2) become the harbingers of life's brevity; Carmen curlers in the company of crucifixes are emblems of worldly vanity rather than useful beauty aids (fig.3); a protective hockey helmet becomes a spectre of what might happen were it not worn; and so on. The compositions as a whole act as allegories of the challenges that face our world with its dwindling resources.

Fig. 2
Plastic Vanitas ~ Still Life with Clocks
[AIBDC, 554, CR, 143, Shelf 7 of 8, 3.7kg]

Curator's overview

As an organisation devoted to learning, we are pleased that the collaboration has been mutually developmental. Neudecker often realises her 3D imagery in plastics. Working with the MoDiP collection has increased her understanding of the potential of this materials group. Creating work with support from the University's photography students has enhanced her understanding of the technological aspects of digital photography. Known for her reinventions of Romantic landscape, still life is a new genre in her repertoire.

After exhibition at the AUB's TheGallery, Plastic Vanitas will be presented in a variety of contexts. At Bow Arts' Nunnery Gallery it will fit into a larger programme about materials that, like plastics, were invented in the Lower Lea Valley. At Bath Spa University's Corsham Court it will be shown alongside the extraordinary Wunderkammer collection with its fossils and stuffed animals recalling the contents of vanitas paintings; and at Poole's Lighthouse it will further integrate MoDiP with our local community.

I should like to thank the artist, our partners and the Arts Council England for their parts in enabling the MoDiP collection to be thus transformed and made visible through art.

Professor Susan Lambert

Curator's overview

Fig. 3 detail
Plastic Vanitas ~ Still Life with Carmen Curlers and Billiard Ball
[PHSL, 1, MS, 1, Shelf 1 of 5, 2.6kg]

Rescued from Oblivion:
On Neudecker's Photographs
Hanneke Grootenboer

Rescued from Oblivion: On Neudecker's Photographs
Hanneke Grootenboer

Fig.4 detail
Plastic Vanitas ~ Still Life with Chopping Board & Cup
[AIBDC 535, CR, 134, Shelf 6 of 8, 1.8kg]

One of Mariele Neudecker's most exemplary still-life photographs shows a tabletop, partly covered with a striped tablecloth, set against a dark background (fig.4). A few objects have been arranged in a pyramidal composition on the right side of the table. From the top left corner, a shaft of light enters the pictorial space, illuminating the display. Neudecker speaks the language of still life fluently. We, as viewers, are quite at home within this careful placement of objects surrounded by silence. We recognise the way the tabletop presents itself as a stage, and appreciate the theatricality of the spotlight. Obviously, the middle objects play the main part, the ones on the side are in supportive roles, and a few extras have been added as well. Neudecker's series and her photographic idiom borrow freely from the rich, venerable tradition of still-life painting.

Upon closer inspection, however, we may be slightly bemused by the kind of objects represented here. Are these plastic cups on the right - objects we never really notice when sipping bad coffee from them - actually worth looking at? What about the green cutting board, the multi-coloured straws in their transparent box, the plastic picnic bowls?

In still-life painting as we know it, objects are usually either symbolic - a timepiece or a skull reminds us of death, a withering flower tells us that all beauty will eventually decay - or very valuable. Seventeenth-century Dutch artists such as Willem Kalf or Jan Davidsz de Heem created meticulously rendered images of rare or otherwise wonderful objects: expensive Chinese porcelain, golden goblets, rich tapestries, or exotic fruits. Their paintings brought together curious objects from the four corners of the world for the viewer to marvel at. In contrast, Neudecker's photographs show us objects that we rarely take the time to look at, and only occasionally admire. After all, these are all disposables, by definition seldom if ever kept, made of the inexpensive materials that are so ubiquitous in contemporary life. Indeed, most of the things we see in Neudecker's

Fig.5 detail
Plastic Vanitas ~ Still Life with Ketchup Bottle and Lemon
[AIBDC, 92, CR, 31, Shelf 7 of 8, 0.8kg]

images are disposables. A cup or a straw is usually thrown away after being used just once. While a cutting board generally survives for a year or two, it, too, will eventually be replaced by another inexpensive plastic object, not meaningfully different from its predecessor. These sorts of objects enter and leave our lives on a daily basis: they form one of the foundations of our most basic activity (feeding ourselves) but they never secure a place within our lives: we throw them out before we take the time to look at them. It is in Neudecker's picture that they gain existence as things as such. Their emergence within the photograph makes us think about them as different entities: as trash now worthy of contemplation. Even more profoundly we realise, staring at this picture, that Neudecker's photographic series has a deep link with the still-life tradition that has inspired it. Most traditional still-life paintings are vanitas images reminding the deeply religious viewers of earlier centuries that despite worldly pleasures of exquisite food and other luxuries enjoyed by the privileged, death was the great equaliser. Earthly pleasures were futile in light of the eternal life in store for every devout Christian. Different as Neudecker's photographs are from these earlier images, their subject is essentially the same: the futility of the plastic cup's life, projected against the

spectacular waste that we produce. What does a cup or straw offer us in terms of luxury and gratification that justifies this waste? In many ways, in Neudecker's photographs plastics are an equaliser in much the same way as death, and we could say that MoDiP basically has rescued these objects from oblivion. It is in Neudecker's photographs that they start their other lives as meaningful objects. The importance of collection is underscored in the image of the assembly of ketchup containers in all their variety: small, large, fat, slim, some flasks taking on different identities as tomato, sausage, banana, or fish (fig. 5). By squeezing too many containers onto a table's surface, Neudecker has turned them into hilarious and endearing objects all the while signifying their immense waste. How many were not rescued and now reside in landfills?

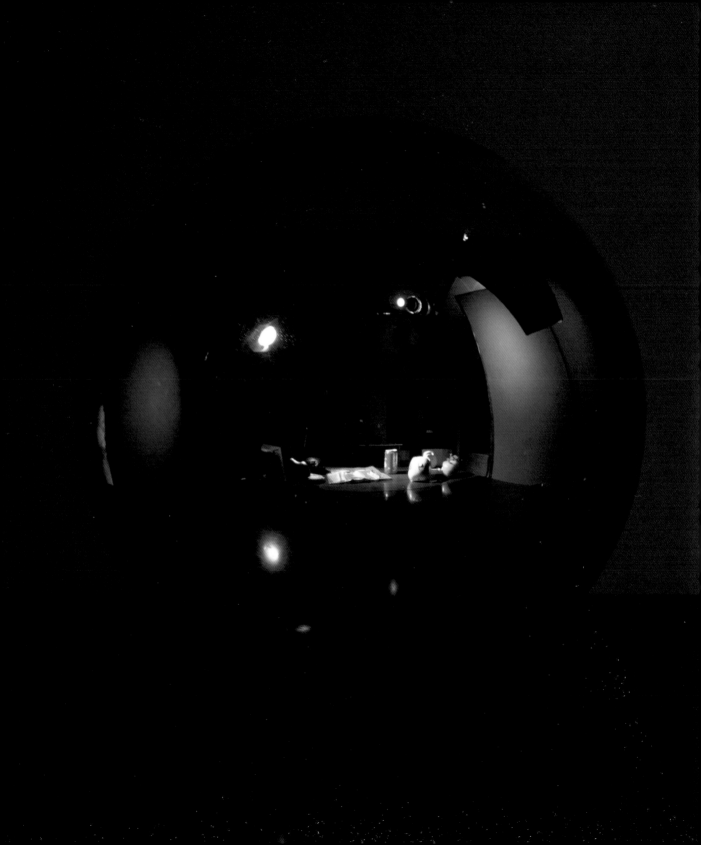

Rescued from Oblivion: On Neudecker's Photographs

Photography's uses of the genre of still life have very productively explored the contrasting meanings of futility and vanitas. In her series *Hardly More than Ever: Photographs 1997–2004*, Laura Letinsky created tabletops not filled with food but scattered with leftovers, while Sam Taylor-Johnson's video *Still Life* (2001) records the process of decay of a bowl of fruit. Both Letinsky and Taylor-Johnson in fact show us what traditional vanitas images are capable only of hinting at: the moment after. The flowers will wither, the fruit will rot, insects will nibble at leaves: everything will turn to dust. Ashes to ashes: this is still life's promise, but only with the emergence of photography and video has it been able to show this fully. Could we say that photography and video, in fact, continue a project that still-life painting started, but in another medium? What do Neudecker's photographs actually do with the genre of still life? And what does it show us?

One of the photographs gives us – literally –a deeper reflection on the process of producing an image (fig.6). In a large globe-shaped lampshade set against an almost black background we peep into an accidental 'still life scene' at the other end of the table bearing the vase. It is hard to tell whether we see another arrangement of plastics, or the leftovers of a lunch: the red object reminds us of a can of Coke. This image strongly reminds us of a famous still life by Pieter Claesz, *Vanitas* (1630) (fig. 7), which displays a violin propped up on some books and a skull, which are surrounded by a timepiece, a quill-and-ink set, a reversed glass, and a large, mirroring orb. In its reflection we see the interior of the room in which the table stands, its window

Fig.7
Pieter Claesz, Vanitas, 1630
© Germanisches National Museum

clearly visible. And just below the window we find Pieter Claesz himself, who is standing behind the easel in the process of painting the scene that we see. It is as if Claesz wanted to show his viewers what the other side of the still life looked like. By including himself in his creation, he made not only himself, but the process of creation as such part of the vanitas message. However, his presence gives the vanitas message a twist. Claesz's picture contradicts the message it clearly aims to convey for not everything has turned to dust. While Claesz himself is long dead, his painting has survived its maker. The reflection makes us aware that this painting, these objects, will also survive us, following the Latin motto, well known in Claesz's time (and not unknown even in ours), vita brevis ars longa: life is short but art endures.

Likewise, Neudecker's photographs provide us with contrasting messages of the destructiveness of waste and a celebration of what has survived this waste. More sustainable than many plastic things, the photograph holds up a mirror to us, and makes us aware of the way we mindlessly throw out the crisps' plastic wrappers. In addition, the very act of photographing plastic things has provided them with an identity, a role in our domestic sphere, and a shape in our imagination. They even get a face. In fig. 8 a combination of cheap kitchen utensils turns into a circus act. Are they performing for us, or set out there to actively return our gaze and make us see them not for what they are but what we do with them? Neudecker's photographs articulate this ambiguity: the glasses, the clocks, the bakelite bowls and boxes seem as much to be looking at us as we are looking at them. The next time we sip bad coffee or suck on a straw, we will pause, hold these objects up to our eyes, and remind ourselves of what we do with their colourful lives. And with ours.

Professor Hanneke Grootenboer

Fig.8
Plastic Vanitas ~ Still Life with Potato Peeler and Lemon Squeezer
[AIBDC, 447, CR, 103, Shelf 6 of 7, 2.4kg]

A Matter of Life and Death
Rachel Withers

A Matter of Life and Death
Rachel Withers

In the midst of life, we are in death – and maybe nowhere more so than in the field of museology, where a good deal of the critical discussion ends up taking a dialectical turn in general, and focusing on dialectics of life versus death – preservation versus decay, reanimation versus mortification – in particular. Are museums places where cultural artefacts are kept alive, or put to death?

Theodor Adorno's early 1950s essay *Valéry Proust Museum* has gained the status of an *Ur*-text in this debate. To try and compress its labyrinthine argument into a few sentences is to run a risk, but here goes. In the blue corner, Adorno's Valéry deplores the museum's babel of competing artefacts. It forces the viewer 'to apprehend in the same moment a portrait and a seascape, a kitchen and a triumphal march'; it is like listening 'to ten orchestras at once'. Incompatible styles go to war with one another and the result is aesthetic carnage. The museum becomes a metaphor for 'the anarchical production of commodities in fully developed bourgeois society,' extrapolates Adorno. Over in the pink corner, Adorno's Proust relishes the museum in the same way a gardener delights over her well-constructed compost heap. Artistic styles and schools 'devour each other like micro-organisms and insure through their struggle the survival of life.' The needs of the present – the imaginative misinterpretations of living viewers, maybe – win out over historical fastidiousness and the 'objective demands' of the museum's holdings gain a second life.

Fig.9
Plastic Vanitas ~ Still Life with Hockey Helmet
[Single Object, 006419, CR, 223, 8 of 8, 1.2kg]

A Matter of Life and Death

A Matter of Life and Death

Mariele Neudecker's doings at the Arts University Bournemouth's MoDiP evidently relate to this discussion in enjoyably twisty ways. Here we have a contemporary artist with a well-established interest in the reanimation of historic high-cultural paradigms (romantic landscape, the Sublime) on the prowl with her camera, stalking the stores of a museum devoted not to fine art but anonymous, handcrafted domestic objects (the 'natural plastics' that make up the Worshipful Company of Horners' collection) and the fruits of mass production (the MoDiP and Plastics Historical Society's collections). Thus, this museum is hardly a 'metaphor' for 'the anarchic production of commodities' within emerging and modern capitalism but a straightforward repository of thousands of those commodities (if such an archive can be straightforward: probably not). For *Plastic Vanitas*, Neudecker has selected, arranged, lit and photographed selected museum items, disguising them as Dutch Golden Age still lifes. Further, she has paid particular attention to objects that evoke the iconography of vanitas and memento mori paintings – at least, in so far as the mostly modern holdings of the Museum have allowed. A terrifying hockey helmet stands in for a skull (fig. 9), and a kitsch doggie figurine for a fine lady admiring herself in the mirror (fig.10); and none of the collection's lemons could be shown dangling an elegant corkscrew of peel (à la Pieter Claesz, let's say) because they are all of the 'Jif' squirty screw-top variety – no peeling required (fig.11). Neudecker's project has lent the museum's often very 'low', disposable-seeming

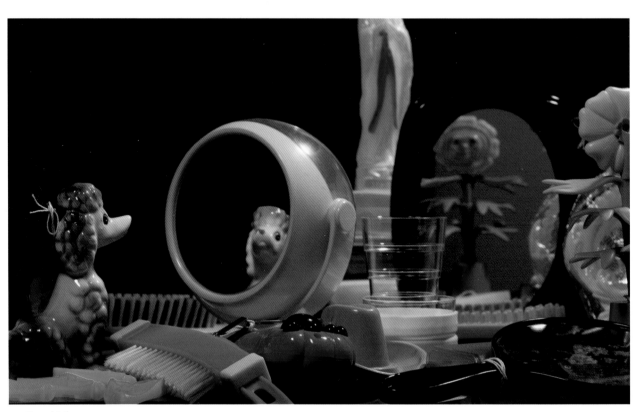

Fig.10 detail
Plastic Vanitas ~ Still Life with Flower and Poodle
[AIBDC, 237, CR, 90, Shelf 2 of 8, 3.8kg]

A Matter of Life and Death

commodities (yogurt pots, door handles, pop bottles, ashtrays, shoe trees, samples of Formica, etcetera, etcetera) the sheen of canonical high culture. However the new identity and status she has given them is a vulnerable one too, since the vanitas formula is generally agreed to be a precarious synthesis of another, this time seventeenth-century, quasi-dialectic that, in vulgar terms, runs as follows:

[luxury goods + affluence + capitalist accumulation = very good, whoopee!]
v.
[luxury goods + affluence + capitalist accumulation = very bad, path to damnation.]

Again, this is a matter of life and death. Is it better to party down in this existence, or hold out for the definitive good time in the hereafter?

Should immersion in immediate experience trump reflection, interpretation, the understanding of the meanings and consequences of experience? In fact, this is not solely a moralistic question posed by the vanitas genre, it is also a museological-cum-curatorial issue. Nicholas Serota probed it in his 2000 Walter Neurath Memorial lecture, entitled *Experience or Interpretation: the Dilemma of Museums of Modern Art.* His discussion intersects with the Valéry-Proust dialectic without exactly reproducing it; it also indirectly relates to one of the larger recent art-historical debates in the field of seventeenth-century Dutch painting.

Fig.11 detail
Plastic Vanitas ~ Still Life with Lemon and Apples
[AIBDC 653, CR, 159, Shelf 6 of 7 1.5kg]

A Matter of Life and Death

In the 1980s, scholars E. de Jongh and Svetlana Alpers went head-to-head over the question of the relative importance of iconographic reading-in (interpretation) versus vision (immediate perceptual experience) for the understanding of Dutch genre. De Jongh argued that Dutch viewers of the time would have construed still lifes as complex encodings of social, moral and theological messages. No, countered Alpers: they reveal an emergent empirical, early scientific attitude; they are inventories arising from a world-view fascinated by the data of sensory experience.

So are still-life paintings inventories of visual experience or ethical narratives demanding decoding and interpretation? Through a clever working constraint, Neudecker has organized *Plastic Vanitas* around this very dilemma. Firstly, she examined MoDiP's holdings to identify specific objects fitting the iconography of the vanitas genre. Next, she retrieved the boxes in which these particular objects resided. For the most part, the boxes contained many items in addition to the one she was after, but her self-imposed system required her to show each box's entire contents, and not just the target object, in her finished composition – no matter how eccentric the consequences. Thus, her vanitas pictures are both a direct document of experience, and an

exercise in the manipulation of symbols: paradigmatic, at the level of inventorying the full contents of particular MoDiP storage boxes, and syntagmatic, at the level of organising 'sentences' of objects via the compositional grammar of the vanitas genre. And with the basic syntax in place, unexpected items of vocabulary are readily interpreted. What could be more natural than the inclusion of the fascia of an automatic gear lever in a vanitas image (fig.12)? Cars are a dangerous and wasteful temptation, gears can fail, driving is bad for you, this object is a warning. Q.E.D.

Neudecker plans to install her mini-museum of the neo-vanitas in a salon-style hang. Row on row, the old and the new, the small and the large, the cheap and the classy, the handmade-unique, the mechanically reproduced and the digitally reproducible,

Fig.12 detail
Plastic Vanitas ~ Still Life with Desk Calendar and Coathanger
[AIBDC, 313, CR, 191, Shelf 6 of 7, 3kg]

Fig.13 detail
Plastic Vanitas ~ Still Life with Bottle Warmer and Yellow Duck
[AIBDC, 77, CR, Shelf 5 7 of 8, 0.8kg]

jostling together: the horror of Adorno's Valéry would surely have been total. Adorno's Proust, on the other hand, might just have got it, but the display would have placed his metaphorical organicism under strain. Maybe he too would have shrunk from this sombre, melancholy, absurd array of (mostly) imperishable, quasi-immortal plastic odds and sods. At present, it seems likely that this species of object will outlive our own. Maybe the hilarious, slightly creepy, yellow bird-shaped drink bottle in one of Neudecker's compositions (fig.13) is reflecting along similar lines. With its little boggling eyes rolling heavenwards in the manner of the figure of Faith in Vermeer's allegory (to pick a painting that is not short of vanitas imagery), it is contemplating a long, lonely hereafter with no humans around to give it a sense of purpose and direction in life. *Vita et ars brevis,* plastics *longa*, as one might say.

Rachel Withers

Ars Longa Vita Brevis? Art is long, Life is short?
Alice Sharp

Ars Longa Vita Brevis? Art is long, Life is short?
Alice Sharp

To contribute an essay on plastics and sustainability to Mariele Neudecker's new exhibition of works for MoDiP might seem like a contradiction. In fact her new work exploring the vanitas painting tradition through creating contemporary still lifes from the museum's collection of plastic items gets to one of the cruxes of sustainability. Will the way we live and the objects we use to live, enable us to live the way we do and prosper in future generations?

Sustainability and plastics

Plastics have brought many benefits. Their lightness is especially advantageous. Their use, for example, in place of metal and glass in vehicle construction means vehicles use less fuel and pollution is reduced. Their use in packaging perishable goods improves their lifespan. Durable and flexible plastic pipes prevent water leakages. Plastics are also an enabler for other materials: for example, combined with woven carbon fibre they create a material of unusual directional strength and stiffness. They also play a significant role in medical surgery. Medical polymer extrusions are capable of existing and being absorbed by the body at a pre-determined rate. Plastics also provide parts for the generation of renewable energy and insulation, which reduce carbon emissions.

However, our current usage is not sustainable. The amount of plastics produced between 2000-2010 is similar to the amount that was made in the whole century that preceded this one.

The major problems are: the waste caused, mainly ending in landfills; the plastic islands floating around our oceans; the leaching of chemicals; ingestion by wildlife, and so from animals to humans. Scientists have collected up to 750,000 bits of micro plastic in a single square kilometre of the 'Great Pacific Garbage Patch'. The US Ocean and Atmospheric Administration's Marine Debris Program has estimated that it would take 67 ships one year to clean up less than one per cent of the North Pacific Ocean.

A major problem is packaging, most of which is not recycled. Although only about 4% of the earth's oil production creates plastics, we cannot keep this level of fossil fuel use and use of hydrocarbons and also combat climate change. We can reduce our use of plastics, increase recycling, reduce littering and increase green chemistry life-cycle analyses but this will not be enough. We must reduce our demand: our current use and disposal are not sustainable.

Contemporary art and plastics

MoDiP is extremely interesting as a context for contemporary art. Many artists including Neudecker use plastic or plastic based materials such as fibreglass in their work (fig. 14). Considering a 'museum' of plastics enables a wider exploration of the role of plastic in our society and how it has changed since plastic was first invented.

Contemporary artists have also used the effects of plastics on the environment as the source of ideas. Studio Swine UK artist-architect collaboration has created the wonderful *Sea Chair*, a stool made on a fishing boat from sea plastic. Plastic bags have been used to raise environmental

Ars Longa Vita Brevis? Art is long, Life is short?

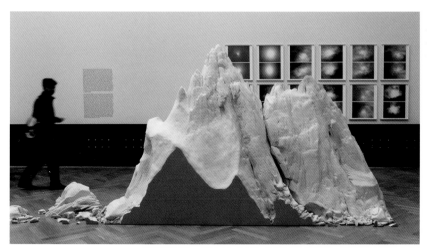

Fig.14
There is Always Something More Important 2012
fibre glass, pigment, plywood
2 channel video on monitors, looped
65cm x 207cm x length 460cm
installation @ 'MODEL - Models in Contemporary Art',
Galerie Rudolfinum Prague, Czech Republic, 2015

concerns by both Cameroonian artist, Pascale Marthine Tayou, who creates enormous vortex installations and Argentinian artist, Tomás Saraceno, whose *Museo aero solar* is a flying museum, a solar balloon completely made up of reused plastic bags.

Mariele Neudecker

Neudecker's work has a timeless quality that references both the past and the future. She plays with our perceptions, distorting dimensions and scale to create sublime landscapes and a version of reality slightly different from our own. Although Neudecker uses a broad range of media including sculpture, installation, drawing and film, photography is central to her practice and she has an ongoing interest in optical devices and the technology of viewing.

Previous to *Plastic Vanitas* Neudecker has explored human impacts on the ocean through collaborating with marine biologist Professor Alex Rogers, Oxford University, set up through my own organisation Invisible Dust. Invisible Dust enables artists and scientists to work together to explore the environment. Rogers highlights that even in the deep sea 3000m below the surface scientists have found plastic. Neudecker created videos *For Now We See* which linked the human sounds of clocks, heart beats and helicopters to scientists' footage of lobster pots, cables and fishing nets in the vast abyss of the deep sea (fig. 15).

For *Plastic Vanitas* Neudecker's ideas first formed when she was visiting Tanzania (February 2014), where she photographed Amani, a semi-abandoned, formerly colonial, research station suspended in limbo between remote, colonial botanical and later medical research, and the future developments into an outpost for Dar es Salaam University. The arrangement of medical and office set-ups were untouched since many years. Coincidentally the scenes were lit directly from a sunlight source on the top as so often

Ars Longa Vita Brevis? Art is long, Life is short?

in vanitas paintings (fig.16). Neudecker soon realised that the real human life and death history of the place that she documented alluded to and emphasised the themes of decay and death in vanitas.

Neudecker has reflected that working on the MoDiP project has made her reconsider plastics and their relationship to the environment. The process of creating the work seems also to echo ideas around sustainability. Much discussion is concerned with the measurement of carbon footprints and what the actual resources are that humans really need to live. In *Plastic Vanitas* Neudecker had a precise system based on the fact that the collection's storage is predominantly determined by weight with lighter boxes on high shelves and heavier ones lower down. For each image she decided to use the entire contents of the chosen box. Neudecker wanted to represent the collection, as it is stored but re-represent it in a new way.

When we see the arrangement of objects in her photographs we are looking at objects that have been apparently randomly gathered together in a single box, the groupings reflecting practical rather than intellectual imperatives: the weight of the 'group of objects' and their coordinates on the shelves feature as part of the subtitle linked to each 'frame'.

So we see in her photographs a number of objects that examine our notions of what plastic is and how we use it. Her system reflects how we, as a society, are measuring the life and sustainability of objects. As those

Fig. 15
Horizontal Vertical (4 of 5) 2013
5 channel video installation with sound
[developed with Oxford University Marine Biologist, Dr. Alex Rogers and Invisible Dust, London]
For Now We See installation at 'British Science Festival' at Church of St Thomas the Martyr, Newcastle, 2014

Fig. 16
Amani Still Life (Office) 2014
giclée print on archive paper
Amani Research Centre, Tanzania - research project: 'African Futures: Archives, Lives, and Hopes
for Science ', lead by Professor Wenzel Geissler, University of Oslo and Cambridge

artists who painted in the vanitas tradition explored, art bears out the
truth of the aphorism at the title of this essay, since most art today, as
in the past, will exist longer than the artist that created it. Neudecker's
still lifes add an extra dimension. They also challenge the way we live,
asking us to think about whether the way we live can be long lasting.

Alice Sharp

Plastic Vanitas
Mariele Neudecker

Plastic Vanitas ~ Still Life with Face Shield
[Single Object, AIBDC 007106, CR,273, shelf 3 of 8, 0.4 kg]

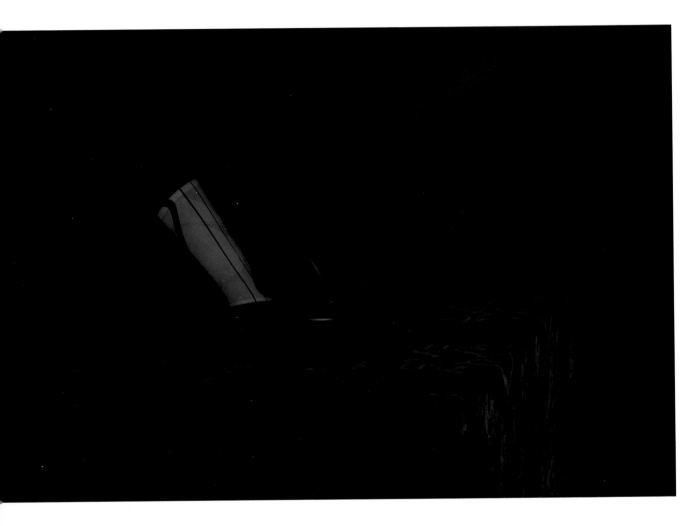

Plastic Vanitas ~ Still Life with Measuring Spoons and Two Snowmen
[AIBDC, 311, CR, 127, Shelf 7 of 8, 1.4kg]

Plastic Vanitas ~ Still Life with Lampshade and Butterfly
[AIBDC, 203, CR, 76, Shelf 4 of 8, 1.1kg]

Plastic Vanitas ~ Still Life with Salt and Pepper Mill
[AIBDC, 562, CR, 151, Shelf 6 of 7, 1.2kg]

Plastic Vanitas ~ Still Life with Thermos Jug and Door Handle
[AIBDC, 316, CR, 192, Shelf 7 of 7, 4.4kg]

Plastic Vanitas ~ Still Life with Ram's Head Snuff Box
[Single Object, WCHL 252, MS, MS, Shelf 1 of 6, 3.4kg]

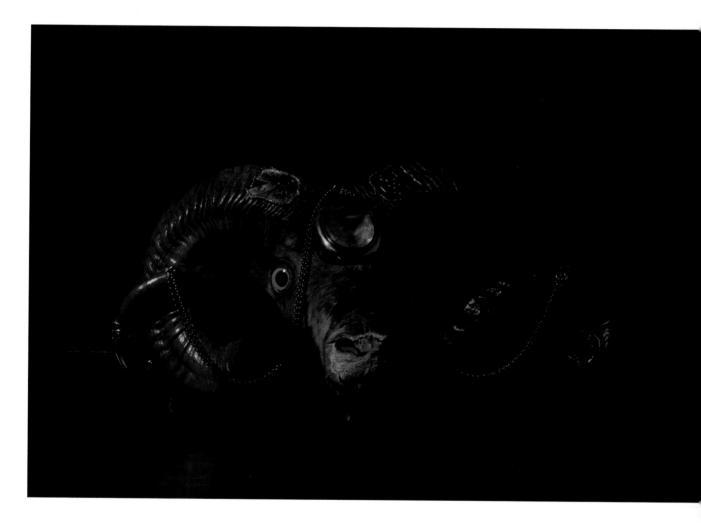

Plastic Vanitas ~ Still Life with Horn Pitcher and Hammer
[WCHL, 15, MS, 34, Shelf 3 of 6, 1.1kg]

Plastic Vanitas ~ Still Life with Hair Comb and Cup Set
[WCHL, 18, MS, 27, Shelf 2 of 6, 2.7kg]

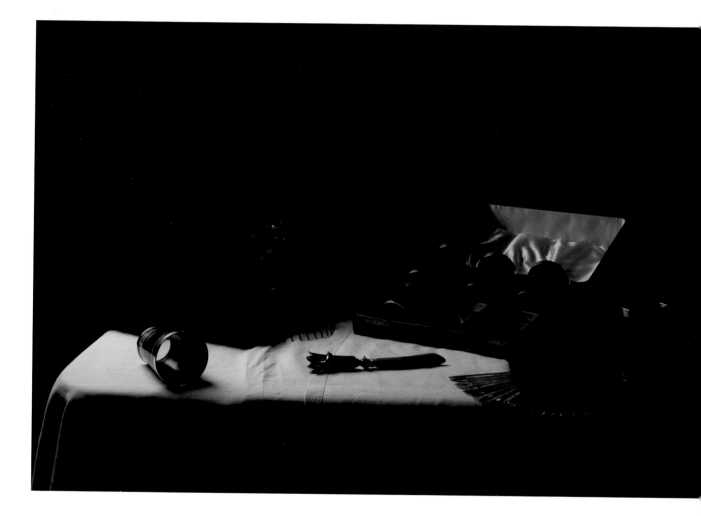

Plastic Vanitas ~ Still Life with Ice Bucket and Torch
[AIBDC 13, CR, 5, Shelf 5 of 8, 2.5kg]

Plastic Vanitas ~ Still Life with Bottle Warmer and Yellow Duck
[AIBDC, 77, CR, Shelf 5 7 of 8, 0.8kg]

Plastic Vanitas ~ Still Life with Snuff Box and Scales
[WCHL 15 MS 34 3 of 6 1.1kg]

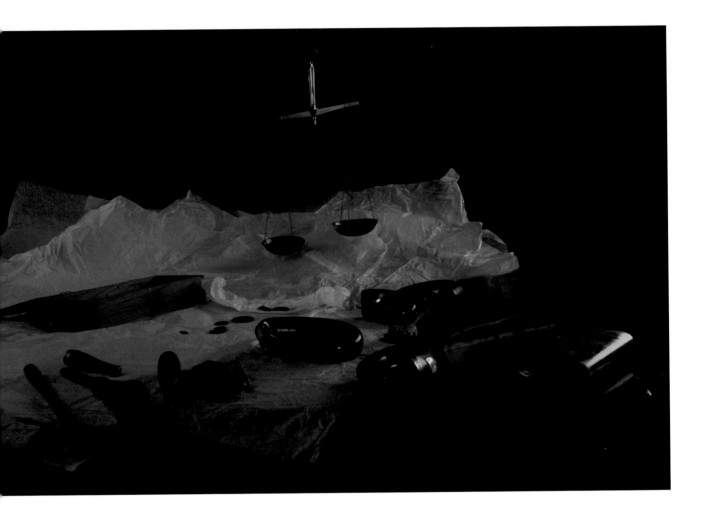

Plastic Vanitas ~ Still Life with Snuff Box and Manuscript
[WCHL 9, MS, 34, Shelf 3 of 6, 0.7kg]

Plastic Vanitas ~ Still Life with Ming Bowl Stacks
[2 Single Objects, Grey and Red, 007007 and 007036, CR, 163, Shelf 1 of 4, 3.2kg]

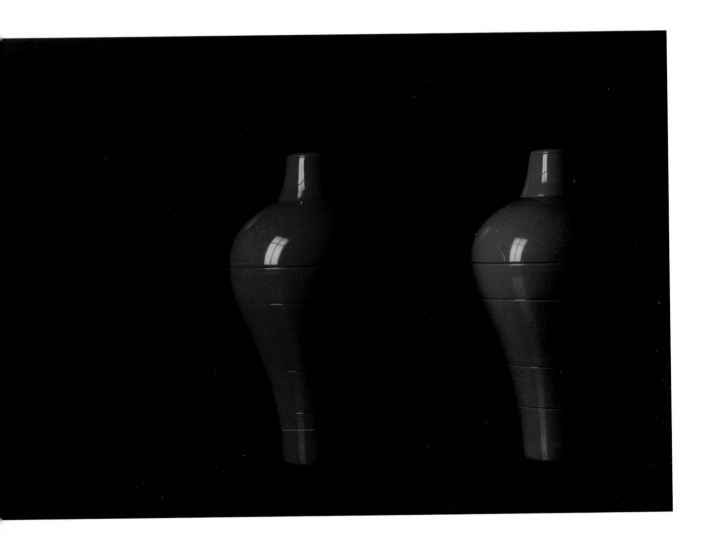

Plastic Vanitas ~ Still Life with Shanghai Vase and Flowers
[Single Object, 006876, CR, 186, Shelf 1 of 7, 2.5kg]

Plastic Vanitas ~ Still Life with Candle Stick and Duck
[AIBDC, 66, CR, 28, Shelf 4 of 8, 2.7kg]

Plastic Vanitas ~ Still Life with Hockey Kit
[AIBDC, 642, CR, 136, Shelf 8 of 8, 1.1kg]

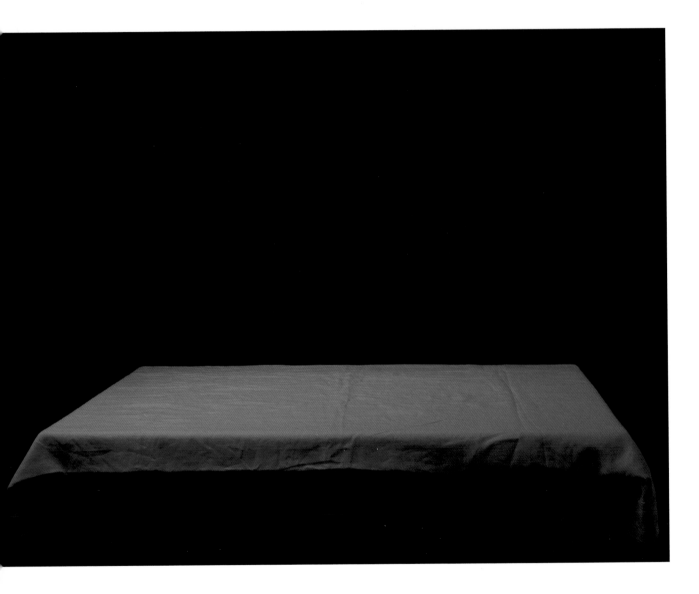

Contributors

Contributors

Mariele Neudecker
Internationally renowned artist Neudecker is a Research Fellow at Bath Spa University. German-born, she studied at Goldsmiths College and Chelsea School of Art and Design, and now lives and works in Bristol. Her work examines the Contemporary Sublime. She focuses on overlaps and coincidences of physical, chemical and psychological realms that are manifest in objects, images and language.

She was short-listed for the Fourth Plinth in 2010 and has shown in Biennales in Japan, Australia and Singapore. Her solo exhibitions include Ikon Gallery, Tate St Ives and Tate Britain in the UK as well as Hinterland at Kunstmuseum Trondheim, Galerie Haas, Zurich, Switzerland and *There is Always Something More Important*, Galerie Barbara Thumm, Berlin. She was selected to present as part of the Antarctic Pavilion: ANTARCTOPIA, Venice Architecture Biennale 2014. In 2015 she showed video installations during *On Light* at the Wellcome Trust in London.

Hanneke Grootenboer
Hanneke Grootenboer is a Professor of the History of Art and the Head of the Ruskin School of Art at the University of Oxford. She is the author of *The Rhetoric of Perspective: Realism and Illusionism in Seventeenth-Century Dutch Still Life Painting* (UP Chicago, 2005) and *Treasuring the Gaze: Intimate Vision in Eighteenth-Century British Eye Miniatures* (UP Chicago, 2012, Kenshur Prize, 2014). Currently, she is working on a book entitled *The Pensive Image* about painting as a mode of thinking, and the way art shapes thought. Her articles have been published in *The Art Bulletin*, *Art History*, and *Oxford Art Journal*, among other venues. Her research interests further include the history of pictorial light after photography; still life and animation; intimate forms of portraiture; the nature of artistic research; the sublime in still life painting; wax-works; and the early modern doll's house as a space for reflection.

Susan Lambert
Professor Susan Lambert is Head of the Museum of Design in Plastics (MoDiP: www.modip.ac.uk), Arts University Bournemouth. In 2006 the University's Management commissioned her to undertake an options review of what was then known as the Design Collection Museum and, as a result, in 2007 MoDiP became the only accredited museum in the UK with a focus on plastics. She and the MoDiP team have organised a large number of exhibitions which demonstrate the contribution of plastics in the 20th and 21st centuries. She leads the Plastics Subject Specialist Network and is a committee member of the Plastics Historical Society. Previously she worked at the Victoria and Albert Museum (V&A), where key roles included Keeper of the Word & Image Department and Head of Contemporary Programmes. The latter involved the initiation, development and instigation of museum-wide avant-garde and interactive programmes to engage new audiences including *Friday Late, Fashion in Motion*, and *Give & Take*. Her publications include *Form Follows Function, Design in the 20th Century* (V&A 1993); 'Plastics – Why not?' in *Extreme collecting; challenging practices for 21st century museums* (Berghahn Books 2012).

Alice Sharp
Alice Sharp, curator and director, set up Invisible Dust, an art and science organisation, in 2009 involving leading artists, scientists and creative technologists in producing exciting commissions exploring the environment and climate change. Previously, as an Independent curator, she managed the Fourth Plinth programme with Antony Gormley and Yinka Shonibare in 2008, the Big Chill Art Trail from 2006 to 2009 and co curated Journeys With No Return, an international touring exhibition to Istanbul, Berlin and London, 2009 to 2010. She won the 2014 PEA (People Environment & Achievement) Guardian UK Arts, Fashion, Music & Film Award, which recognises the crucial contribution of inspirational people who are making a difference to the green agenda.

Invisible Dust presents artworks made with scientist collaborations to large audiences at events such as the British Science Festival, National Maritime Museum, Euro Science Open Forum together with public art projects such as *HighWaterLine Bristol* in 2014, a 32 mile long chalk drawing by community members to highlight flooding by Eve Mosher. In 2015 Adam Chodzko will create an intriguing and challenging experimental new film *Deep Above* to explore behavioural psychology of climate change and why we are failing to act in anticipation of the November 2015 UN International Panel on Climate Change Climate Conference (IPCC).
www.invisibledust.com.

Contributors

Rachel Withers

Rachel Withers is Senior Lecturer in the History and Theory of Art and Design, Bath Spa University. She holds degrees in Fine Art and Critical Studies, and the History of European Art and Architecture. She teaches at Bath School of Art & Design at Bath Spa University. A frequent contributor to Artforum International, Withers has also written for the *Guardian*, the *New Statesman*, and many other mainstream and specialist art publications, including the catalogues of the Venice and Sydney Biennials and the first *Tate Modern Handbook*. She is Secretary of the UK Branch of AICA, the Unesco-sponsored international organization for art criticism, and has served on the juries of various national and international art awards, including the Max Mara Art Prize for Women and the International Awards for Art Criticism. In 2007 Dumont Verlag published her illustrated monograph on Swiss artist Roman Signer, and she has also published key texts on the works of Susan Hiller, Mike Nelson, Joao Penalva, and performer/choreographer La Ribot. In spring 2015, her project Roman Signer's *Library of Marvels (Fast Version)*, preliminary findings from her research in Signer's personal library, was on show at the Rose Lipman Building in Hackney, London.

List of Works

List of Works
Commissioned by the Arts University Bournemouth, courtesy: the artist and Galerie Barbara Thumm.

1   Plastic Vanitas ~ Still Life with Clocks
[AIBDC 554, CR, 143, Shelf 7 of 8, 3.7kg] p. 9

giclée print on archive paper, 240 x 360 mm, edition of 5 plus 2 a/p's

2   Plastic Vanitas ~ Still Life with Carmen Curlers and Billiard Ball
[PHSL 1, MS, 1, Shelf 1 of 5, 2.6kg] p. 11

giclée print on archive paper, 193 x 247 mm, edition of 5 plus 2 a/p's

3   Plastic Vanitas ~ Still Life with Chopping Board and Cup
[AIBDC 535, CR, 134, Shelf 6 of 8, 1.8kg] p. 14

giclée print on archive paper, 356 x 546 mm, edition of 5 plus 2 a/p's

4   Plastic Vanitas ~ Still Life with Ketchup Bottle and Lemon
[AIBDC 92, CR, 31, Shelf 7 of 8, 0.8kg] p. 15

giclée print on archive paper, 405 x 570 mm, edition of 5 plus 2 a/p's

5   Plastic Vanitas ~ Still Life with Mirror Ball
[Single Object, AIBDC 005555, CR, 102, Shelf 5 of 7, 1.3kg] p. 16

giclée print on archive paper, 463 x 415 mm , edition of 5 plus 2 a/p's

6   Plastic Vanitas ~ Still Life with Potato Peeler and Lemon Squeezer
[AIBDC 447, CR, 103, Shelf 6 of 7, 2.4kg] p. 19

giclée print on archive paper, 357 x 318 mm, edition of 5 plus 2 a/p's

7   Plastic Vanitas ~ Still Life with Hockey Helmet
[Single Object, AIBDC 006419, CR, 223, 8 of 8, 1.2kg] p. 22

giclée print on archive paper, 408 x 574 mm, edition of 5 plus 2 a/p's

8   Plastic Vanitas ~ Still Life with Flower and Poodle
[AIBDC 237, CR, 90, Shelf 2 of 8, 3.8kg] p. 24

giclée print on archive paper, 375 x 590 mm, edition of 5 plus 2 a/p's

9   Plastic Vanitas ~ Still Life with Lemon and Apples
[AIBDC 653, CR, 159, Shelf 6 of 7 1.5kg] p. 25

giclée print on archive paper, 500 x 750 mm, edition of 5 plus 2 a/p's

10   Plastic Vanitas ~ Still Life with Desk Calendar and Coathanger
[AIBDC 313, CR, 191, Shelf 6 of 7, 3kg] p. 26

giclée print on archive paper, 285 x 420 mm, edition of 5 plus 2 a/p's

11   Plastic Vanitas ~ Still Life with Bottle Warmer and Yellow Duck
[AIBDC 77, CR, Shelf 5 7 of 8, 0.8kg] pp. 27 45

giclée print on archive paper, 380 x 560 mm, edition of 5 plus 2 a/p's

12   Plastic Vanitas ~ Still Life with Face Shield
[Single Object, AIBDC 007106, CR,273, shelf 3 of 8, 0.4 kg] p. 36

giclée print on archive paper, 490 x 730 mm, edition of 5 plus 2 a/p's

13   Plastic Vanitas ~ Still Life with Measuring Spoons and Two Snowmen
[AIBDC 311, CR, 127, Shelf 7 of 8, 1.4kg] p. 37

giclée print on archive paper, 311 x 512 mm, edition of 5 plus 2 a/p's

14   Plastic Vanitas ~ Still Life with Lampshade and Butterfly
[AIBDC 203, CR, 76, Shelf 4 of 8, 1.1kg] p. 38

giclée print on archive paper, 200 x 290 mm, edition of 5 plus 2 a/p's

15   Plastic Vanitas ~ Still Life with Salt and Pepper Mill
[AIBDC 562, CR, 151, Shelf 6 of 7, 1.2kg] p. 39

giclée print on archive paper, 210 x 320 mm, edition of 5 plus 2 a/p's

16   Plastic Vanitas ~ Still Life with Thermos Jug and Door Handle
[AIBDC 316, CR, 192, Shelf 7 of 7, 4.4kg] p. 40

giclée print on archive paper, 385 x 577 mm, edition of 5 plus 2 a/p's

17   Plastic Vanitas ~ Still Life with Ram's Head Snuff Box
[Single Object, WCHL 252, MS, MS, Shelf 0 of 6, 3.4kg] p. 41

giclée print on archive paper, 456 x 640 mm, edition of 5 plus 2 a/p's

18   Plastic Vanitas ~ Still Life with Horn Pitcher and Hammer
[WCHL 15, MS, 34, Shelf 3 of 6, 1.1kg] p. 42

giclée print on archive paper, 314 x 469 mm, edition of 5 plus 2 a/p's

19   Plastic Vanitas ~ Still Life with Hair Comb and Cup Set
[WCHL 18, MS, 27, Shelf 2 of 6, 2.7kg] p. 43

giclée print on archive paper, 570 x 830 mm, edition of 5 plus 2 a/p's

20   Plastic Vanitas ~ Still Life with Ice Bucket and Torch
[AIBDC 13, CR, 5, Shelf 5 of 8, 2.5kg] p. 44

giclée print on archive paper, 444 x 610 mm, edition of 5 plus 2 a/p's

21   Plastic Vanitas ~ Still Life with Snuff Box and Scales
[WCHL 15 MS 34 3 of 6 1.1kg] p. 46

giclée print on archive paper, 500 x 740 mm, edition of 5 plus 2 a/p's

22   Plastic Vanitas ~ Still Life with Snuff Box and Manuscript
[WCHL 9, MS, 34, Shelf 3 of 6, 0.7kg] p. 47

giclée print on archive paper, 250 x 420 mm, edition of 5 plus 2 a/p's

23   Plastic Vanitas ~ Still Life with Ming Bowl Stacks
[Single Objects, AIBDC 007007/007036, CR, 163, Shelf 1 of 4, 3.2kg] p. 48

giclée print on archive paper, 210 x 310 mm, edition of 5 plus 2 a/p's

24   Plastic Vanitas ~ Still Life with Shanghai Vase and Flowers
[Single Object, AIBDC 006876, CR, 186, Shelf 1 of 7, 2.5kg] p. 49

giclée print on archive paper, 310 x 463 mm, edition of 5 plus 2 a/p's

25   Plastic Vanitas ~ Still Life with Candle Stick and Duck
[AIBDC 66, CR, 28, Shelf 4 of 8, 2.7kg] p. 50

giclée print on archive paper, 440 x 650 mm, edition of 5 plus 2 a/p's

26   Plastic Vanitas ~ Still Life with Hockey Kit
[AIBDC 642, CR, 136, Shelf 8 of 8, 1.1kg] p. 51

giclée print on archive paper, 480 x 715 mm, edition of 5 plus 2 a/p's

27   Plastic Vanitas ~ Empty Still Life with Large White Cloth, p. 52

giclée print on archive paper, 510 x 655 mm, edition of 5 plus 2 a/p's

28   Plastic Vanitas ~ Still Life with Lantern
[Single Object, WCHL 239, MS, MS, Shelf 0 of 6, 1.4kg]

giclée print on archive paper, 416 x 610 mm, edition of 5 plus 2 a/p's

List of Works

29 Plastic Vanitas ~ Still Life with Lola Lampshade
    [AIBDC 483, C,R 181, Shelf 4 of 7, 0.6kg]

    giclée print on archive paper, 300 x 440 mm, edition of 5 plus 2 a/p's

30 Plastic Vanitas ~ Still Life with Desert Bowl Set and Hoof Protector
    [PHSL 7, MS, 3, Shelf 3 of 6, 3.9kg]

    giclée print on archive paper, 575 x 860 mm, edition of 5 plus 2 a/p's

31 Plastic Vanitas ~ Still Life with Shoe Horn and Flute
    [PHSL 14, MS, 7, Shelf 2 of 5, 2.1kg]

    giclée print on archive paper, 390 x 580 mm, edition of 5 plus 2 a/p's

32 Plastic Vanitas ~ Still Life with Three Thermos
    [AIBDC 13, CR, 5, Shelf 5 of 8, 2.5kg]

    giclée print on archive paper, 268 x 335 mm, edition of 5 plus 2 a/p's

33 Plastic Vanitas ~ Still Life with Copper Shade and Cloths
    [Single Object, AIBDC 005554, CR, 102, Shelf 5 of 7, 1.3kg]

    giclée print on archive paper, 397 x 588 mm, edition of 5 plus 2 a/p's

34 Plastic Vanitas ~ Still Life with Map
    [Single Object, AIBDC 006762, CR, 178, 0.1kg]

    giclée print on archive paper, 400 x 578 mm, edition of 5 plus 2 a/p's

35 Plastic Vanitas ~ Still Life with Sewing Kit and Butter Dish
    [AIBDC 313, CR, 191, Shelf 6 of 7, 3kg]

    giclée print on archive paper, 320 x 480 mm, edition of 5 plus 2 a/p's

36 Plastic Vanitas ~ Still Life with Shovel and Scales
    [AIBD 222, CR, 84, Shelf 4 of 8, 1.4kg]

    giclée print on archive paper, 210 x 275 mm, edition of 5 plus 2 a/p's

37 Plastic Vanitas ~ Still Life with Moon Bowl
    [Single Object, AIBDC 006875, CR, 187, Shelf 2 of 7, 2.1kg]

    giclée print on archive paper, 292 x 394 mm, edition of 5 plus 2 a/p's

38 Plastic Vanitas ~ Still Life with Salad Servers and Rubik's Cube
    [AIBDC 147, CR, 39, Shelf 7 of 8, 2.1kg]

    giclée print on archive paper, 302 x 429 mm, edition of 5 plus 2 a/p's

39 Plastic Vanitas ~ Still Life with Tape Rack and Clocks
    [AIBDC 37, CR, 17, Shelf 1 of 8, 2.7kg]

    giclée print on archive paper, 248 x 330 mm, edition of 5 plus 2 a/p's

40 Plastic Vanitas ~ Still Life with Pineapple and Blue Cloth
    [AIBDC 133, CR 37, Shelf 5 of 8, 2kg]

    giclée print on archive paper, 270 x 360 mm, edition of 5 plus 2 a/p's

41 Plastic Vanitas ~ Still Life with Camera and Inkwell
    [AIBDC 171, CR, 65, Shelf 1 of 8, 4.1kg]

    giclée print on archive paper, 240 x 320 mm, edition of 5 plus 2 a/p's

42 Plastic Vanitas ~ Still Life with Bourgie Lamp
    [Single Object, AIBDC 006874, CR, 165, Shelf 2 of 4, 3.4kg]

    giclée print on archive paper, 500 x 750 mm, edition of 5 plus 2 a/p's

43 Plastic Vanitas ~ Still Life with Parkesine Nitrocellulose and Light Blue
    [PHSL 28, MS, 10, Shelf 5 of 5, 0.9kg]

    giclée print on archive paper 435 x 590 mm, edition of 5 plus 2 a/p's

44 Plastic Vanitas ~ Empty Still Life with Tablecloths and Fur Coat

    giclée print on archive paper, 300 x 440 mm, edition of 5 plus 2 a/p's

45 Plastic Vanitas ~ Empty Still Life with Two Cloths

    giclée print on archive paper, 270 x 380 mm, edition of 5 plus 2 a/p's

46 Plastic Vanitas ~ Empty Still Life with Lace Tablecloth

    giclée print on archive paper, 184 x 253 mm edition of 5 plus 2 a/p's

47 Plastic Vanitas ~ Empty Still Life with Blue Cloth

    giclée print on archive paper, 210 x 275 mm, edition of 5 plus 2 a/p's

48 Plastic Vanitas ~ Empty Still Life with Orange Cloth

    giclée print on archive paper, 431 x 532 mm, edition of 5 plus 2 a/p's

49 Plastic Vanitas ~ Empty Still Life with Flowers

    giclée print on archive paper, 355 x 460 mm, edition of 5 plus 2 a/p's

Acknowledgements

The artist and the MoDiP team would like to thank David Hazel, Course Leader, BA Photography, and Tom Preston, Principal Technician, Photography, from the Faculty of Media and Performance, and their students, especially William Ablett, Leo Gauvain, Molly Howells, Kieran Hughes, Joana Picolo de Sousa, Adam Roberts and Emma Webster for the sharing of their expertise and assistance with this project. Special thanks go to Julio del Castillo Vivero, who additionally spent time making an animation of all the images taken in the process of making Plastic Vanitas.

The artist would also like to thank the MoDiP team: Susan Lambert for curating the project, Pam Langdown, Louise Dennis and Katherine Pell, for helping to select the boxes photographed and organising the residency on a day to day basis. Also she would like to thank John Taylor at Bath Spa University for carefully and patiently printing the images; Andrew Short, Leigh Tunnadine and Roy Carder for taking great care with all the framing; Sally Hope, for her sensitive design of the publication; the writers Hanneke Grootenboer, Alice Sharp and Rachel Withers, for their thoughtful contributions to this book; Violet McClean, Senior Gallery Officer, for managing the preparation of the work for display and its installation in TheGallery, AUB.

Thank you all.

Arts University Bournemouth

Arts University Bournemouth is the leading professional arts university dedicated to turning creativity into careers. Established in 1885, AUB is based on a single campus where students and staff come together to innovate, collaborate and connect across art, design, media and performance. For each of the last ten years, AUB has been in the top 10 of all UK universities for employability (DLHE). aub.ac.uk

TheGallery, established in 1998, at Arts University Bournemouth (AUB) offers a unique space in the South West for the arts including design, media and performance. It is a major resource for contemporary visual art at the University and has received national and international recognition.

text + work is a gallery initiative that invites artists to develop exhibitions and events. This has forged partnerships with writers and critics who provide supportive narrative in the form of published text to accompany the exhibitions.

Plastic Vanitas was developed in partnership with Bath Spa University, which has given additional support, Bow Arts' Nunnery Gallery and Poole Lighthouse.

Supported by Arts Council England

Cover
Plastic Vanitas - Still Life with Copper Shade and Cloths
[Single Object, 005554, CR, 102, Shelf 5 of 7, 1.3kg]

  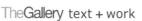